# HOW TO BE SUCCESSFUL AT INTERVIEWS

## An In-Depth Guide on Interviewing Answering Questions and Putting Your Best Foot Forward

BY

**ERNEST ENABULELE**

# DISCLAIMER

The information presented in this report solely and fully represents the views of the author as of the date of publication. Any omission, or potential misrepresentation of, any peoples or companies, is entirely unintentional. As a result of changing information, conditions or contexts, this author reserves the right to alter content at their sole discretion impunity.

The report is for informational purposes only and while every attempt has been made to verify the information contained herein, the author assumes no responsibility fqor errors, inaccuracies, and omissions. Each person has uni ue needs and this book cannot take these individual differences into account.

# Table of Contents

# INTRODUCTION

You attend college with the hopes and dreams that you will get a job upon graduation. Thousands of others are doing the same thing, which can make applying for jobs tough. If you turn in an application, it is possible that 20 to 30 others have as well. The worst part is most of them will have the same experience and qualifications that you have. So, how can you become the standout candidate if everyone has reviewed the same material and prepared? Is it possible to ensure that you are memorable?

The answer is yes, it is possible. This eBook is directed to those who are applying for jobs and want an edge in the interview stage. When you know the tips and tricks to use during an interview, you can walk in there more confident. Confidence leads to immediately standing out and having the ability to answer all types of questions.

It has become standard practice for any job seeker interested in how to prepare for an interview to visit the website of a potential employer. When you are looking for a job, your success is determined by your job interview techniques and how much knowledge you have about your potential employer. This knowledge is critically important because many of us make the mistake of confusing how much we know about our profession or industry with our knowledge of that particular company.

While this can be an understandable mistake, as it can be very difficult to find information on some employers, conducting some background research on the company where you want to work will help you to avoid one of the most common mistakes made in job interviews.

You should aim to learn as much as possible about the company before you meet with a potential employer. You can research aspects such as the industry in which the company operates, sales volume, finances, its main competitors and its business objectives. Understanding the history of the company and the business model is important to understanding its strategy, style, and its general approach to problems and their solutions.

The key to success is to treat the interview as a project, for which you must gather information, make decisions on feasibility, set objectives, identify the resources needed, draw up a plan of action, and manage the project carefully through to closure. In simple terms, you must be professionally prepared for the interview, in order to have the optimum chance of success.

It is common for candidates to have questions asked that they are not comfortable answering. The questions may not always have an easy answer, and you need to think carefully prior to answering them. These are the times when it is good to know how to deal with the situation, what to say, and how to remain composed. The tactics you will learn in this book will help you face all sorts of situations you may face in an interview.

In this eBook, we will be discussing more on how to become successful at interviews.

Let's begin!!!

# CHAPTER 1

# INTERVIEW SUCCESS SECRETS

A few things to keep in mind during an interview include:

- What to wear
- Proper preparation for the interview
- How to handle the tricky questions
- Drafting the perfect resume
- What to say during an interview
- How to read the interviewer

All of these points mentioned are vital in assisting a candidate to face everything that may come up during an interview. You can find answers online, but the answers may not be reliable to better your chances.

# Different Types of Interviews

There are five basic types of interviews, but they all require an interviewer and the interviewee (you). The questions and interview setup will vary between the different types.

The interview styles include:

- Phone Interview
- Video Interview
- Panel Interview
- Exit Interview
- Lunch Interview

## Phone Interview

Many view phone interviews as informal, but they make just an impact on the job process. In fact, interviewees make some of the most critical mistakes during a phone interview. Phone interviews are growing in popularity, so it is important to know how to handle them.

- Phone interviews save time for both parties, which make them ideal for career fairs.
- Companies like to call potential employees prior to having a physical interview.

- Interviewers can cover any questions from the application prior to the formal interview.
- Interviewees can discuss the position and have any questions answered.

There are drawbacks to phone interviews, with the primary concern being that it only caters to the needs of the employers. Candidates can be caught off guard and it may come when conditions are not favorable. Phone interviews are best when they are scheduled, so the candidate can be prepared.

## Video Interview

Thanks to new technology, video interviews are becoming more popular. They are mainly used in the first interview stage, to help the interviewer narrow the candidates. They are also common in positions that are virtual, where calling someone into the office is not possible. Some of the things to keep in mind with a video interview include taking them as seriously as an in- person interview.

- Be in a location where you can be professional.
- Make sure you have everything set up early enough to be situated for the interview.

- Dress professionally, from head to toe.
- Always keep eye contact with the camera so you are talking to the interviewer.

Video interviews require a lot more planning than a phone interview, and they can be difficult to ensure proper set up. You can secure a successful interview by treating it like an in-person interview and checking the interview equipment a day before the actual interview.

## Panel Interview

Panel interviews are held as a primary selection process. A candidate is brought in front of a group of interviewers. They will be taking notes and chatting throughout the interview. This interview is extremely stressful and it can be nearly impossible to get a good read on the interviewers. There are a few things that can be done to prepare for a panel interview.

- Bring a clean sheet that contains the highlights of what you wish to mention during the interview. Focus only on the key assets; do not write an essay. Create an outline of what you want to be mentioned and keep it brief.

- Prepare by knowing the interviewers or bringing paper to take note of names. When you refer to the interviewer by the name they prefer, it is more likely they will remember you. It also lets them know that you are paying attention and directing a reply.

- A beneficial tip is using the last question you were asked as a cross-reference with other questions you have been asked before. This keeps you in tune with where the interview is going and will help you remain calm. It will also allow you to talk to more than one interviewer at once.

- Always have a notepad with you during a panel interview. It is likely that you will be given bits of information that will be worth remembering. It also shows the interviewers that you are paying attention and care about the job. You can use the notes you take as a way to remember information that may be brought up later.

- It is vital that you make eye contact during a panel interview. It can be difficult to figure out whom to look at, so the best tactic is to start with the person who asked the question and then span the panel.

The hardest part of a panel interview is feeling outnumbered. You need to focus on the questions when your mind is trying to impress multiple people. The best way to remain calm during the interview is to realize that panel interviews are often done with candidates they view as strong possibilities. They take a great deal of time to consider the candidates and you simply need to show why you are the most qualified. By staying calm and considering the questions before answering, you can successfully complete the interview.

## Lunch Interview

Lunch interviews are very laid back, but should still be taken seriously. They are usually used as a final talk prior to the hiring process. It is very common for interviewers to be very frank with the candidate. In response, the candidate is expected to be relaxed and answer the questions as if they would if they were talking to a friend. However, lunch interviews are not easy because it is hard to be confident when someone is watching you eat. In addition to contemplating your answers, you must also make sure you are thinking about eating politely.

- Order something simple to eat that you can break down and take small bites. Bread is always a safe choice.
- Stick with water because it does not stain. It is never a good idea to order alcohol, even if the interviewer does.
- Order something in close comparison to the interviewer (including in price).
- Always wipe your mouth with a napkin and never order food that will likely be stuck in your teeth.
- Try to order food that can be eaten with a fork, unless it is a small sandwich. Most companies pay for the lunch meal, but always be prepared to pay your own way. It is also a good idea to bring enough money to cover the interviewer's meal and the tip.

After the interview, make sure you thank the interviewer and offer a firm handshake. Finally, follow-up with a thank you letter that will give the interviewer another reminder of who you are.

## Exit Interview

Exit interviews are usually held when a person is leaving a company. Some companies do not use exit interviews, but those who do are looking to build relationships with former employees. It is important to remember that the interviews can be used for possible restructuring of the policies and procedures. Exit interviews can happen any time between the last final days of employment up to two or three months after the final date of employment.

**Advantages to Exit Interviews**

- Helps focus on policies and procedures that mayhave become outdated
- Help determine the employee's state of mind in quitting
- Gives a safe place for future re-employment or discuss difficulties
- Can identify possible departmental competencies
- Identifies conflicts and complications that can be harmful to other employees or management

**Disadvantages to Exit Interviews**

- Personal conflicts and gossip can cloud discussions

- Tough to maintain a positive environment, especially if the employee was fired
- Provides a time for disgruntled employees to voice their anger, which can be disruptive to the workplace

# Skill Building

Skill building is an important part of being successful in an interview. It is not something that can be taught in a college class. You can only be successful with skill building by using the knowledge that you have obtained over many years. It does not require a person to be super smart or high caliber. You simply need practice and patience to allow your skills to build. Some important aspects to consider include building your writing skills.

Writing skills are the only way to succeed in today's job force because the Internet is crucial to all companies. You will want to show that you know how to type and how to communicate. This can be done through crafting resumes, cover letters, thank you letters, and blogs. Make sure you remain up to date on newsworthy topics by reading magazines, news sites, or news blogs. There are several RSS feeds that you can subscribe to that will keep you updated.

In addition to writing blogs, you can be noticed by your participation on social networks. You want to use the networks to see how others succeed or trip up. Interact with people, build networks, and take the time to build your skills.

# Tools and Miscellaneous Things to Have

When you are preparing to job hunt, you will want to have some tools that will help you prepare. Some items can be pricey, but they will pay for themselves when you get a job. The biggest thing the tools do is by making you look more professional.

## Must Haves:

1.      Laptop/Computer – You could borrow one to get your work done, but buying is a better option. You will need a computer or laptop to create your resume, cover letters, reference pages, and any samples if necessary.

2.      Internet Access – Most companies post their job openings online. You will want to make sure you have an updated copy of your resume on any job hunting sites that you can think of. Make sure you check the resume regularly to ensure the information is ready if a job opens.

3.      Briefcase or Portfolio– You will need a way to transport your paperwork to and from job fairs and

interviews. Briefcases and/or portfolios will allow you to look professional while keeping everything protected.

4. Mobile Phone - Mobile phones allow you to be accessible at all times. If you post your jobs in several places, then you will want to make sure that the potential employers can reach you. Smartphones will also offer you the ability to check on jobs on the go.

# Significance and Importance of the Right Resume

In order to start on the right food with an employer and secure an interview is with a good resume. Most companies will use the resume as a way to get a good feel for a candidate. You want to make sure your resume is effective, concise, and leaves a positive impression with the employee. You do not want a prebuilt resume that took you only a couple minutes to create because the employer can see right through it. Several things MUST be kept in mind while writing your resume.

Never, ever lie on the resume Mention all skills, qualifications, experiences, and awards carefully Make your resume relevant to the job you are applying to Keep a resume simple and look at creating a few customized resumes for different industry types you are applying for.

There are various formats available for resumes, including ones for fresh graduates to list their degrees and awards. Candidates that have been employed in other jobs will want to focus on their previous work experience. With all types of resumes, you want to make sure it is very easy to read. Most employers are skimming over resumes so you want short sentences and bullet points. Use tables and correct terminology whenever you can.

You want the resume to promote yourself without sounding as if you are boastful. Work on emphasizing your skills and experience. In addition to promoting yourself, select references that can be reached and are willing to verify your information. Make sure your references know that they may be contacted so the employer does not catch them off guard. Remember that the possible employer is looking at your resume for character and personality purposes, but they will also look at your grammar and spelling to see how well you can write and communicate.

# CHAPTER 2

# PREPARING FOR AN INTERVIEW

Proper preparation for the interview is vital when it comes to applying for a job and attending an interview. In addition to knowing what to say, you will gain confidence when you practice. You will be calm during the interview and be prepared for bizarre questions. There are multiple ways to prepare for an interview, but a few will give you the best chance of success.

- Talk to family and friends – The best way to prepare for an interview is to talk to a person who has been through the interview process. Find out what advice or tips they have to offer, and see if you can find out what mistakes they experienced. Using their mistakes qas a way to learn how to perfect your interview techni ues will give you a better chance of preventing errors.

- Go social – Talk to people in your community or on a forum that would be willing to give you tips on preparing for an interview. Some great people to talk to include guidance counselors, professors, former classmates, and people who may be working for the company you are interested in. Many companies will reward employees for referrals, so make sure you note that on your resume, cover letter, or in the interview.

- Use career sites – Websites such as LinkedIn or Employment Solutions Network are great resources for interview prepping. Job fairs are another way to meet companies and have impromptu interviews. Always carry your resume and cover letters on you when you attend a job fair so you can hand the paperwork to the employer when asked.

# How Does Appearance Aid?

Appearance plays a huge part in helping secure a job. Candidates want to look their best when talking to a potential client. This can include dressing nice, but it may also include shaving and removing any piercings.

Remember that first impressions are lasting and you want them to look at your resume at least. You want to create a lasting impact with your appearance and walk when approaching a company representative.

- Practice your walk and handshake the night before your interview, preferably in front of a mirror.
- Answer questions in front of a mirror so you can monitor your facial expressions. You do not want to be overdramatic, but you want your face to add to the answer.
- Keep your business clothes prepared and ready every day.
- Do not buy a new outfit the day before an interview because it might be uncomfortable. Practice in your interview outfit so you are comfortable. Ties are a very nice touch, as are buffed shoes.

- Females should avoid wearing multiple jewelry pieces. You want to present yourself to the interviewer, but you want to make sure it is not over the top and scares them off.

- Do not have a complete makeover prior to the interview. You want to be comfortable withq your looks so you appear relaxed while answering uestions.

- Make sure you sleep well the night before and practice good hygiene on the morning of the interview.

# Tips to Prepare – Pre-Interview

The pre-interview is the period right before the interview and when most people get a sour stomach. Feeling stressed and tense is very common, and it makes sense as to why.

However, some things can be done to help prepare for the interview day.

- Know the location of the interview and practice getting there during different traffic types. Make sure you are aware of where there is parking so you can get to your interview on time.

- Know the answers to common questions and make sure you have done your research on the company. You want to show that you care about the company.

- Have planned answers for uncommon questions such as favorite color or animal. Companies use these questions to see you think on your feet and handle unusual situations.

- Attempt to arrive about ten minutes before your interview and always greet the receptionist.

- Do not smoke before or during an interview.

- Make sure you have gone through the bathroom and all of your electronics are put on mute so you can give the company your undivided attention.

# Self-Introduction: Your Key to Interview Success

Once you have been invited to an interview you must get ready to create the image of someone they will surely want to hire above all other job applicants. Everybody has an opinion as to how you do that, but what do you actually do and what do you say? Self-introduction is your key to interview success because you are starting from a baseline position where they have no experience of who you are or what you are like.

Yes, they should have read your resume and cover letter you sent in, but that only gave them enough for them to want to see you in person. Now you are going to meet the hiring manager in person, you have a one-off make or break opportunity to get them to see you as the only person they want to employ.

As you know, interviewers will often rely heavily on their first impressions, to the extent that the interview becomes merely a confirmation of that first impression, either good or bad. So if self-introduction is your key to interview success, the first and most important aim is to create a positive first impression. Everybody has an opinion as to how you do that: look 'em in the eye, give 'em a firm handshake, speak up and don't mumble; know your stuff. All good ideas, but what do you actually do and what do you say?

## Create A Favorable First Impression

The way to create a favorable first impression is to be sure you appear confident and open. When you meet your interviewer for the first time, make eye-contact at the introduction and repeat the interviewer's name as you shake hands and thank them for inviting you to the interview. As you get seated, smile to indicate you are ready to get down to business.

What often follows is the invitation to 'tell them about yourself' which allows you to commence your self-introduction that is so important to your interview success. This is the phase where you develop the rapport that will carry you through to the positive outcome at the end of the interview.

Because self-introduction is your key to interview success, you must have previously prepared exactly what you are going to say. This is not some long story about your life, but a short focused statement that sounds interesting to the listener. You make it interesting by keeping it short (less than 3 minutes) and by showing that you are interested in both the job and the organization. This means you need to do some research about the business beforehand.

## Strengths and Achievements

In your self-introduction, you will include some examples of your strengths and achievements which relate directly to the requirements of the new job. This must also demonstrate your personal qualities that you apply when you are doing the job because the type of person you are is often far more important than just having the ability to do a job.

The way you outline your self-introduction, in particular, the way you speak, tells the interviewer whether you are confident in your abilities so you must rehearse it well, but don't try to be what you are clearly not - you'll only be found out at a later date. Get a friend to listen to your self-introduction with a critical ear because if it sounds false it will set the alarm bells ringing with the interviewer who will detect that it is not the real you and destroy the rapport you were buildingq up. Practice speaking faster or more slowly, louder or uietly and try to vary it throughout.

When you have prepared your self-introduction, ask yourself this question: 'What does the interviewer need?'

The answer is that the interviewer needs to identify the best candidate to hire, whilst keeping the costs to a minimum and the fewer people interviewed the better. The need is alsofor the person who appears to be the best 'fit' in terms of both personality and technical ability. Also remember that they may need to justify their decision to hire you, to someone higher!

Prepared well, this self-introduction is your key to interview success because it helps to create that all-important first impression, helps you to build the rapport with the interviewer and satisfies the questions about whether you are the sort of person who will fit into the organization successfully.

# Traditional Vs Competency Based Interviewing

## Traditional Interviews

Traditional interviews generally use broad-based questions and are often paired with behavioral interview questions into what we would call a new "hybrid" interview.

Success or failure is often based on candidate's ability to communicate and establish rapport. Candidates, be sure to use the job description to assist in tailoring your answers to the job that you are interviewing for. Typical questions in a traditional interview are used to gain insight by reviewing your resume and qualifications.

Here are a few general tips to remember before answering questions:

- Listen carefully. If you feel the question is unclear, ask politely for clarification.
- Pause before answering to consider all facts that may substantiate your response.
- Always offer positive information; avoid negativity at all times.

- Discuss only the facts needed to respond to the question.
- Get directly to the point.
- Focus and re-focus attention on your successes.
- Remember, the goal is not to have the right answers so much as it is to convince the interviewer that you are the right person.
- Be truthful, but try not to offer unsolicited information
- Try not to open yourself to areas of questioning that could pose difficulties for you.

**Traditional questions and how to answer them**

Tell me about yourself?

The response to this question should not be your life story. Giving a very brief personal history is ok. The primary goal is to introduce yourself simply. A successful answer will be demonstrated when you answer this with confidence because you have prepared in advance. Research the job that you are seeking and understand what qualities and experience may be sought-after. Then correlate that to the strengths and expertise that you possess and promote any relevant points. Demonstrating that you are a great match for the job by answering this question right will put you on the fast track to success.

## Why Did You Choose Us?

This question allows interviewers to determine which job seekers want a job or which want to work for the company. This is an opportunity to show off your research. You may respond to current transactions the company may be involved with. If the company is the Cleveland Clinic, you may want to discuss clinical trials or medical break-through recently published.

## What Do You Want out of Life?

Today, many employers are looking for employees who lead balanced lives. Being well rounded and having a good social life outside of work allows you to better deal with potentially stressful situations of the job.

## What are your career goals?

The purpose of this question is to determine if your goals are compatible with the company. This will help the company decide if they can offer you a position in line with your future goals. Always tie your response to the position that you are interviewing for. Stating how your experience and education can be applied to the position is an excellent way to impress the interviewer.

## Competency Interviews

Competency-based interview questions attempt to link together three parameters knowledge, skills, and attitude. These competency-based questions will assess whether you have the right balance between great interpersonal skills, education or experience, and the right attitude for the role in question. To prepare for competency-based interview questions, make a list of competencies that you think are important for the job for which you are being interviewed for.

Look back at the job listing for examples of required skills and attitudes.

Next, list situations in which you have demonstrated each of these competencies.

For each situation, write down the situation or problem, the actions you took to handle the problem, and the ultimate results. Review this list before your interview.

Be prepared to be asked for details, including names, dates, budgets, and outcomes. The interviewers are likely to ask you about lengthy projects you've been involved in you'll need to tell them how your role has evolved and how you handled deadlines, pressures and difficult personalities. When you give examples from your work experience, the interviewer will probe you to try to understand how you think and how you determined what steps to take and in what order.

**Competency questions and how to answer them**

<u>Tell me about a time your communication skills improved a situation</u>

You will be assessed on your abilities to communicate effectively and sensitively and should use an appropriate work-related example, possibly entailing handling disgruntled customers or colleagues and highlighting your excellent listening skills as well as verbal communication skills.

<u>Give an example of a change in the workplace and how you handled this</u>

If you have managed change in the workplace, this is an ideal question to illustrate all your skills and abilities. If not, answer in a way which demonstrates your flexibility and the positive manner in which you meet challenges.

## Give an example of a time you identified a new approach to a workplace problem

This question is a test of your analytical skills and likely to be asked of management candidates who need to prepare a great example which illustrates key skills such as analysis, problem- solving, innovation, and practicality. Candidates for administration-type posts asked uestions of this nature might use simple work-based examples such as when their budgeting skills caused substantial savings in areas such as postal charges, stationery purchases, etc.

## Give an example of team leading in past employment

You should summarize the task and nature of the group but focus primarily upon your role as team leader. List the personal qualities you possess which made you ideal for leading this team and how you achieved success. Conclude your answer by giving examples of the lessons you learned while leading this team.

## How do you cope with adverse circumstances?

This is quite a wide question, and you will need to think carefully about the response you prepare to the uestion. The interviewer will be assessing your coping mechanisms and whether you learned and progressed from your adversity.

# CHAPTER 3

# REASONS WHY PEOPLE ARE NOT SUCCESSFUL AT INTERVIEWS

Landing the interview for that dream job can be an exhilarating ride for anyone seeking a change in their career. The giddy excitement of that chance of being so close can make anyone desperate to do well. However, there are many cases in which those who want to succeed have not, generally because of mistakes made before the interview has even finished.

It is common knowledge that an interviewee should give precise examples of previous work about questions, maintain regular eye contact with their interviewer and arrive on time. However, there are other potential mistakes that you may not realize, which can be avoided.

## Not impressing with your dressing

It is amazing how many applicants really do not consider what they are wearing to an interview. There are those who do turn up to an interview in just jeans and a t-shirt. This does not look professional to the interviewer and can seem like the interviewee has no real intention of pursuing the job. No matter how 'cool' or trendy the organization is, it is always better to be overdressed than underdressed.

It is not just dressing in the right clothes that can make the difference. Having the clothes freshly cleaned and professionally ironed is a huge benefit. Wearing a creased shirt or trousers shows poor organization and a lack of personal care.

## Your lack of passion shows

If you find yourself applying for positions that don't excite you, don't be surprised if potential employers sense this lack of passion. Employers know that skills can always be taught, but that passion is either there or it's not.

If you're genuinely excited about a job, be sure to convey this in your cover letter and interview. Explain your reasons for wanting the position, and share ideas you'll be excited to explore should you get the job.

## Your resume or CV doesn't showcase your value to the company

Your resume is what's going to get your foot in the door. If it isn't accurately showcasing your suitability for the job, you'll never get the chance to impress in an interview.

## You haven't researched the job or company

Employers want to know you took the time to learn a bit about the company. Not knowing the name of the CEO or where the head office is could convey that you're disinterested or even lazy. Take some time before the interview to research the company online. Employers don't expect you to know all the company's inner workings, but you should have a good grasp of publicly available information.

## You're sending the wrong impression

Your interview is your one chance to impress a potential employer. Are you doing any of the following, which could send the wrong impression?

- Arriving too early or too late
- Dressing inappropriately

- Joking around too much or being sarcastic
- Asking about the salary too soon in the interview (leave
- this until last)
- Not showing any personality
- Appearing bored or disinterested during the interview

If you've been job hunting for a while, it may be time to take a step back and ask yourself what you could be doing wrong.

If you're brave enough, email a past interviewer and ask why you didn't get the job--while knowing the truth can be hard, it may help you in the long run.

# How To Sell Yourself At Interviews

Self-marketing and self-promotion make all the difference when you're looking for a job. When you are trying to sell yourself and impress a prospective employer, the first and most important tool you should use to your advantage is your resume and cover letter. Never make the mistake of using another person's resume to make yours. The other person may not have the skills you have, or may not want to highlight certain aspects. By doing so, you are only going to harm yourself and your prospects. You have to make the most of your resume and covering letter, and use it to highlight what you can offer to the company that your competitors cannot.

To know what the perfect resume and cover letter should be like, it would be best to behave like an employer. This is more like role-playing, where you play the role of the employer and ask questions about the resume. This will give you an insight into what to expect at the interview. You get a chance to prepare yourself on the key qualities an employer looks for in an employee; ualities like a degree from a good school or university, good organizational skills to use in the workplace, relevant experience in a particular industry and good writing skills.

Go through a few resumes online, select the ones you most like and study them. Do not copy them exactly, but study them and then frame your resume to reflect the best of those resumes; it really does help to enact an almost real job hunt situation. This is what makes you ready to face the panel and sell your talents to get the best deal possible.

After you have finished playing the role of employer and understood what an employer needs, next play a hardcore salesperson. This is when you really start self-marketing and self-promotion. Most people call it bragging, but you shouldn't be scared by the prospect of self-marketing. It is very important that you do so because this will help create a niche for yourself in the workplace. Marketing is evident in every sphere of life. Study a few of the marketing concepts that are around you and think about which appeal to you and why and use these to sell your skills to the employer. The purpose of self-marketing is to capture attention, hold on it and convince the person that you are what the company needs.

Follow this advice, and you will find out how much more confidence you feel while in a job interview situation. Don't hope you do well in an interview, control the results by preparing yourself to do your best. Present your credentials and experiences as a solution to the job interviewer's immediate employment issues. Do that, and you will increase your odds of finding a career position instead of just another job.

# CHAPTER 4

## LIKELY INTERVIEW QUESTIONS AND ANSWERS

Are you ready to ace your upcoming job interview? It's important to be prepared to respond effectively to the questions that employers typically ask during interviews. Since these job interview uestions are so common, hiring managers will expect you to be able to answer them smoothly and without hesitation.

You don't need to memorize all of your answers, but do think about what you're going to say so you're not put on the spot during the job interview. Your responses will be stronger if you prepare in advance, know what to expect during the interview, and have a sense of what you want to focus on during your interview. Even if you aren't able to recall the specifics of the answers you planned, simply knowing that you prepared will boost your confidence during the interview and help you feel more at ease.

# Top Questions and Answers

Review these top interview questions you'll most likely be asked at a job interview, plus examples of the best answers, so you're prepared for some of the more challenging questions that may come up during the interview.

**Q: Can you tell me about yourself?**

A: In this type of question they aren't asking for an autobiography. IT requires you to focus on your unique selling points that is featured on your CV, application form etc. Keep it professional. Apart from talking about your career, ensure to say something about your education and qualifications including hobbies and interests.

This is one of the first questions you are likely to be asked. Be prepared to talk about yourself, and why you're an excellent fit for the job. Try to answer uestions about yourself without giving out too much, or too little, personal information. You can start by sharing some of your personal interests and experiences that don't relate directly to work, such as a favorite hobby or a brief account of where you grew up, your education, and what motivates you.

If it feels daunting to generate this information from scratch, you can rely on a simple formula to construct your answer. The 'present-past-future' formula is a way to share key background points while ending on a high note. Begin with a brief overview of where you are now (which could include your current job along with a reference to a personal hobby or passion), reference how you got to where you are (here you could mention education, or an important experience such as a past job, internship or volunteer experience) and then finish by touching on a goal for the future.

Bonus points if you're able to identify how the position you're applying for aligns with how you envision your future.

Remember to be careful about what you include in your answer – avoid potentially contentious subjects such as political or religious leanings, unless you are absolutely positive that your opinions would be well-received by your interviewer. You should also avoid talking too much about family responsibilities or hobbies that might make your interviewer wonder whether you could commit yourself 100% to the job.

No matter how you choose to respond, write out your answer in advance and then read it aloud to ensure it sounds natural.

Try to keep it short and sweet, as you don't want to come across as the type of person who endlessly drones on about themselves.

Example: I am a highly driven individual with extensive experience acquired in-sector. I thrive in highly pressurized and challenging working environments.

**Q: Why have you applied for this vacancy? What attracted you to this vacancy? Why do you think you are suitable for this job?**

A: The interviewer wants to know what appeals to you most about the job. Your emphasis should be on demonstrating to the interviewer that you understand what the role entails.

Example: I've applied for this vacancy because it's an excellent match for my skills and experience-and because it represents a challenge which I know I'll relish.

**Q: Why do you wish to leave your current position? Why do you wish to leave your current employer?**

When asked about why you are moving on from your current position, stick with the facts, be direct, and focus your interview answer on the future, especially if your leaving wasn't under the best of circumstances. The interviewer wants to understand your motivation to change jobs. Are you committed to moving to another job?

Always try to put a positive slant on your response; it's better to give the impression that you're more motivated by the possibility of new opportunities than by trying to escape a bad situation. In addition, it's important to avoid bashing your current organization, colleagues or supervisor. An employer is not likely to want to bring on someone who talks negatively about a company.

- A: Seeking greater opportunities
- Seeking further advancements
- Taking a step up the career ladder.
- New challenge.

**Q: Why do you want to work for this organisation? What is it about our organisation that attracts you?**

The interviewer is analysing your motivations and probing your expectations of their organisation. Your focus should be on what attracts you to their organisation.

Example: I want to work for an organisation which is forward thinking and isn't afraid to tackle new challenges.

**Q: What are your strengths? What are you good at?**

A: This is one of the questions that employers almost always ask. When you are asked about your greatest strengths, it's important to discuss the attributes that will qualify you for the specific job and set you apart from the other candidates.

Take the time, before the job interview, to make matches between your qualifications and the requirements as stated in the job announcement. This way, you will have examples ready to hand that will demonstrate your suitability for the job.

Identify what your unique selling points are. Establish if the strengths are relevant to the role they are interviewing for.

It can be helpful to remember the tip to "show" rather than "tell." For example, rather than stating that you are an excellent problem solver, instead tell a story that demonstrates this, ideally drawing on an anecdote from your professional experience.

Example: I am able to demonstrate excellent creative judgement, I am very good at juggling multiple tasks simultaneously in my current role.

**Q: What is your greatest weakness?**

A: Another typical question interviewers will ask, is about your weaknesses. Do your best to frame your answers around positive aspects of your skills and abilities as an employee, turning seeming "weaknesses" into strengths. For example, you might say something like, "I've always struggled with perfectionism – I truly want to do the job correctly the first time, but this sometimes means that I devote more time to a project than is necessary. I've learned to balance this drive with the equally important responsibility of meeting deadlines."

You can also share examples of skills you have improved, providing specific instances of how you have recognized a weakness and taken steps to improve yourself.

**Q: What can you bring to this job?**

The interviewer is, therefore, asking you what your unique selling points is, looking for why you are the suitable applicant than others.

A: If you don't know what is it you are offering then how can you sell yourself effectively to the organisation. Demonstrate that you are capable of going the extra mile.

**Q: Where do you see yourself in five or ten years' time?**

A: Avoid being too specific, present yourself in terms of what level of responsibility, career you will have reached.

Example: Two years from now I expect I will have progressed significantly in my career. I can see that there are indeed a lot of opportunities both for ongoing professional development and promotion.

**Q: In what ways are you a team leader? Can you tell me about a team you worked in and the role you played on that team?**

Answer: Approach the answer from the angle of the job you are applying for, deliver an answer which reflects the type of job.

**Q: How do you handle stress and pressure?**

A: What do you do when things don't go smoothly at work? How do you deal with difficult situations? What do you do when something goes wrong? The best way to respond to this question is to give an example of how you have successfully handled stress in a previous job.

Avoid claiming that you never, or rarely, experience stress.

Not only is this difficult to believe, but it could also lead the interviewer to conclude that you've only worked in low-pressure environments and therefore aren't equipped to handle a difficult situation. Rather, formulate your answer in a way that acknowledges workplace stress and explains how you've overcome it, or even used it to your advantage.

**Q: How would you describe yourself? How would your boss/colleagues describe you? What do you think your references will say about you?**

A: The interviewer wants to see how you perceive yourself, use adjectives like ambitious, determined, highly motivated etc.

Example: I am a positive and enthusiastic person, would describe myself as a highly motivated person and very determined etc

**Q: Do you prefer working on your own or as part of the team? Can you tell me about a team you worked in and the role you played within that team?**

A: The interviewer will be looking at evidence of your abilities

- Ability to recognise and understand the viewpoints of others.
- Communicate effectively with others.
- Example: I believe I have strong communication skills, I enjoy working with others. I'm also good at helping the team to spot mistakes in our approach - and potential problems.

**Q: Do you work well on your own initiative? Are you able to manage your own workload?**

The interviewer is seeking proof that you are such an employee. IT requires more than a one-word answer. I will advise giving example from a past or present job which closely matches the job description will have a huge impact.

Example: I enjoy working with others but I am also able to work on my own initiative. I have a sole responsibility –

**Q: How do you get things done at work?**

A: The interviewer wants to know how you plan and organise yourself to ensure you achieve your objectives.

**Q: What motivates you?**

The interviewer wants to get more information out of you, ensure to give information consistent with the job for which you are applying. I will suggest you cite areas like results and recognition, challenges and also elaborate on these to demonstrate their value to your employer.

Examples: I'm motivated by the zeal of working in a team, I 'm very result-driven. I like to rise to challenge as part of a concerted teamwork.

**Q: When can you start?**

A: Be careful about this question for several reasons:

It doesn't mean that you have "landed the job." They may be just checking to add that to their notes. You must keep your guard up until you are in your car and driving away from the interview.

If you are currently employed, you should be honest about the start date and show professionalism. You should tell them you would have to discuss a transition with your current company to see if they require a two-week notice (or some other timing). If you currently have a critical role, your potential new employer would expect a transition period.

If you can start right away (and they know you are not currently employed), you certainly can say you're able to start tomorrow. The sense of urgency and excitement about starting work at the new company is always a good thing.

**Q: How did you find this job?**

A: You may have found the opportunity through research on ideal jobs where you can make the most impact and hope to grow professionally.

I would also hope you looked for companies that you feel meet your standards for corporate culture, investment in employees, successful business model (or perhaps giving back to the community), and any other aspects you feel are important to you.

Make sure you can go into a little detail on what you found in your research.

The "job" may have found you. In that case, you can say you were contacted by HR or a recruiter who felt you were a good fit. But don't leave it there.

You should still mention you did your homework and verified that this is right for you -- as a potential contributor to the company's success, and as a good match for what you're looking for in an employer.

**Q: Why were you fired?**

A: This is another danger zone. This is not the time for defending yourself with a long story about you being the victim.

If you made a mistake, you are going to have to try to minimize the severity of the situation. An argument with a boss could be described as a difference in opinion. Not following orders because your moral compass told you not to could be described as "taking the high road."

Just be careful not to cast blame on others. Consider including a "silver lining." Did you learn a lot from the experience and now possess knowledge that will mitigate the chances of this happening again?

Laid off is not fired: If you were part of a layoff, this is different from being fired. It was likely a financial decision by management, and you were part of a group that was targeted as part of budget cuts. Layoffs are typically not personal -- they are just business. Hiring managers know this (and likely have been involved in one at some point in their careers).

**Q: Do you have any questions?**

My simple advice is: yes, you had better have questions. When I hired people to work on my teams in the past, I expected interviewees to have uestions.

This is your chance to "interview the interviewer." In essence, to learn about the company, the role, the corporate culture, the manager's leadership style, and a host of other important things.

Candidates, who are genuinely interested in the opportunity, ask these types of questions. Those who don't ask questions give the impression they're "just kicking the tires" or not really too concerned about getting the job.

When given the floor to ask questions, you should realize the interview is not over yet. Good candidates know this is another time to shine.

A: It is imperative that you ask questions that do three things:

1.      Show you did some research about the company.

2.      Mention something else (related, but interesting) about you.

3.      Will have an interesting answer or prompt a good discussion. Close by asking if they have any concerns.

You may not get a chance to address shortcomings in a follow- up interview -- it is imperative to understand what was missing from the discussion while still in the interview. After you have had a chance to ask your questions, you will want to validate that you are an ideal candidate for the job. To do this, you should probe into the minds of the interviewers and see if there are any concerns they have about you.

The key question to do this can be along the lines of:

"After discussing this job, I feel as if I would be a perfect fit for it. I'm curious to know if there is anything I said or didn't say that would make you believe otherwise."

The answer you get to this question may open the door to mentioning something you did not get to talk about during the interview or clarify any potential misconception over something that was covered.

# Competency Interview Questions

Apply STAR to answer scenario questions

S-Situation, T-Task, A-Action, R-Result.

**Q: How do you answer pressure? Can you tell me about a time when you were under pressure and how you handled it?**

Answer

You are expected to talk about a situation where you were under pressure -and how you rose to the challenge.

**Q: Can you tell a time about a time when you have failed to achieve a goal? Can you tell me about a time when you've failed to meet an important deadline?**

The interviewer will be looking at how you deal with adversity and don't give the interviewer the impression that you've never failed.

Example

In my last job I was given a task to submit a report etc

**Q: What's the worst mistake you've made at work and how did you deal with it?**

The interviewer will be expecting a demonstration of how you reacted to your mistake and what action you took to deal with it.

Answer

The crucial aspect is to learn from the mistakes try and place emphasis on the effort you made to resolve the situation.

## Q: Can you tell me about a major work you were involved with that went wrong?

Answer- The interviewer is interested in how you dealt with it. The interviewer wants to ensure that you 're the sort of employee who would be capable of doing that.

## Q: What would you do if you disagreed with a decision taken by your line manager?

The interviewer wants to identify the manner in which you would express your disagreement. Your answer should be around the scenario of a minor disagreement and also place emphasis on how you would use interpersonal skills and communication.

## Q: How did you get your last job?

A: How you were able to convince the employer that you were the right person for the job.

**Q: What changes have you made to your current job role since you started?**

The interviewer is looking for evidence of drive, enthusiasm, and initiative. Describe ways you took other responsibilities that weren't part of your job description.

**Q: What have you learned in your last job? Or in each of your previous roles?**

A: The interviewer is looking at how you have developed professionally whilst working in your last job not expecting you to talk about your responsibilities, duties or achievements.

**Q: Can you tell me about your appraisal? What were areas for improvement identified in your last appraisal?**

The interviewer wants you to talk where there is room in your performance. Be honest and talk about the positive points that were mentioned in your last appraisal and briefly on the less negative points.

**Q: Why are you leaving your job? Why do you wish to leave your current position?**

The interviewer is exploring the reasons why you are leaving?

**Q: Why is there a gap in your CV?**

A: The interviewer will be curious to know the reason why you experienced a period of unemployment. The efforts you have made to get a job.

**Q: Why do you want to work for this organisation?**

The interviewer wants to ensure you understand what their organisation is all about, tell the interviewer the key points you know about their organisation ie source via the website. Communicate effectively how you feel you are suitable for working in such a reputable organisation.

**Q: What appeals to you most about this vacancy? Why have you applied for this vacancy?**

The interviewer wants to know if you fully appreciate what will be involved if you were appointed to the role. To understand the role for which you are applying for.

**Q: How do your skills and experience match the job description/person specification?**

A: The interviewer wants you to explain how your skills and experience match the job description/person specification.

Select a handful of issues and briefly mention about each in turn in respect of your prospective employer's needs.

**Q: What have you learned and how have you developed over the last year/ Two years? What have you learned in your previous roles?**

A: Give examples which are directly relevant to the role you are now applying. As an individual, training you have undertaken to date.

**Q: What is the current headline news?**

A: The interviewer is trying to know how much interest you take in the world around you.

Example: The major news at the moment is –ensure to be current.

**Q: How can you adapt to a new work environment?**

The interviewer wants to know you are prepared to adapt as soon as possible.

A: Please refer to your current or previous job and how quickly you were able to settle in.

Q: **Would it be a problem if we asked you to work overtime/ evenings/weekends?**

A: I'm reasonably flexible if the hospital needs are such that it would be advantageous for me to work long hours including weekends despite my other commitments. I would certainly be prepared to work.

Q: **How do you handle being criticised? Can you tell me about an occasion when your work was criticised?**

A: This will give the interviewer an idea about what sort of person you are to work with.

Q: **what reservations do you have about working for us?**

A: Reiterate what it is that attracts you to this organisation.

Q: **What makes you better than any other candidates we are interviewing? Why should I hire you?**

Are you the best candidate for the job? Be prepared to say why you're the applicant who should be hired. This is not the time to be modest (although neither should you be conceited).

Make your response a confident; concise, focused salespitch that explains what you have to offer the employer, and why you should get the job. This is another good time to review the ualifications and the requirements in the job listing, so you can craft a response that aligns with what the interviewer is looking for.

The interviewer is looking for your USP-Unique selling points why they should be hiring you and not the other candidates. Let the interviewer know how best you match the job description.

**Q: Can you tell me about what you find exciting about your current job? What do you find exciting about your current job?**

A: The interviewer is trying to identifier what you enjoy most and sees how you can be excited about the new position.

# CHAPTER 5

# ANSWERING CHARACTER QUESTIONS

**What do you think of your previous boss?**

Your answer could show you're a team player—or a backstabber.

Whether your previous boss was your best friend or your worst enemy, talking about him or her to a prospective employer takes a little tact. How you describe past relationships speaks volumes about you, not the boss, which is why interviewers pose the question.

Interviewers are looking for a few different things when they ask this question: how well you handle being put on the spot, how well you play with others, and how you like to be managed. Come prepared to answer, so you don't get caught off-guard and say something you'll regret.

<u>Be positive—even if it's difficult</u>

The experts agree that saying something positive about your former boss is the only way to answer this question regardless of your true feelings.

If a candidate rants negatively about a prior manager, the interviewer often considers the employee the problem and will be hesitant to make the hire.

Obviously, if you had a great manager, acknowledge that and specify what made them so great. If, on the other hand, you had a more challenging relationship with your manager, proceed cautiously.

You want to highlight positive aspects of your manager's leadership style and what you learned from him or her. If the interviewer pushes for some sort of criticism, say something that ends on a positive note.

You may want to acknowledge that while you had very different styles, you found a way to work together to deliver results or meet customer needs. Be prepared to give a specific example that can be shared in a positive way.

You say: "My boss was strong-willed, which sometimes made it difficult to communicate new ideas; however, we always managed to talk it out and find solutions that were best for the company."

## Bring it back to your strengths

Your answer to this question can indicate how you like—or don't like—to be managed. How does that match with my own management style? Would this be a relationship that works?

The interviewer may also be testing to see what you'll be like to work with. Will you make a positive contribution to the company's culture, or will you need to be referred?

Whatever the reason, remember they are interviewing you, not your former boss. Keep the focus on what skills and experience you bring to this position. Let your strengths show qin your answer and move the interview onto more important uestions.

You say: "She was so effective at advocating for our department. I learned a lot from her about how to diplomatically manage people, keep communication lines open between departments and how to advocate for the team."

## Demonstrate discretion and loyalty

By asking this question, an interviewer might also be testing you to see how you would handle sensitive inquiries from customers, colleagues or others.

I'm not necessarily looking for loyalty to the boss, but how loyal are they to the organization? When they leave our company will they talk bad about our organization?

Many applicants fail to realize that their criticism of their boss is often perceived as their unwillingness to accept accountability for their own actions.

You say: "We had our differences, but I thought it was important to stay focused on our goals and to set up my manager—and my team—for success."

Know what to leave out

While you should always be honest in a job interview, there are certainly details that don't need to be shared, especially if they have the potential to cast you in an unflattering light.

**What is your salary history?**

Talking too openly about your salary early in the hiring process may eliminate you. Don't say too much too soon.

Asking someone, "How much money do you make?" is considered a rude question in most circumstances. Normally, the answer would be, "Not important ." But when applying for a job, especially one you are interested in, you should prepare for questions about salary.

Recent changes have made it unlawful for employers to ask candidates about their salary history during the screening and interview processes. Massachusetts adopted a salary history ban in 2016 (it will go into effect July 2018); and in 2017, California (in effect January 2018), Oregon (in effect January 2019), Delaware (December 2017), and Puerto Rico (in effect March 2018) did the same.

The best way to deal with the question in a job interview is to defer the subject of your salary history until you have more facts. Take these two examples:

Arlene is applying for a position as director of community relations at a major hospital. The ad asks applicants to include a salary history with their queries. Arlene dutifully adds a salary history to her resume and sends it off.

Debra is applying for the same job. She takes a different approach and writes on the bottom of the cover letter,

"Salary history is confidential information to be supplied in the interview."

In Arlene's case, her letter and salary history will be opened by the receptionist, picked up by the HR coordinator, copied and then sent to the hiring manager for review. The hiring manager will make a judgment based on appropriate experience and salary expectations. If he decides Arlene is not the right fit for the job, he will tell HR he is not interested. By this time, three people will have viewed Arlene's salary history, and she will not even get an interview.

Debra's letter will be handled in the same manner, but the salary history will be missing. Now the hiring manager will have to judge Debra based on her experience and background. He may call Debra and ask for her salary requirements, but she can still postpone the discussion and in uire about the salary range budgeted for the position.

## Consider this first

- Verify the job's scope before you talk about salary. It is difficult to discuss compensation before you have sufficient information about the position and level of responsibility.

- Research the job market before the interview to give you an idea of what the position is worth. You should know the going rate for the same position as a person with your experience and skills.

- Consider the timing. Depending on where you are in the interview process, it is best to delay giving your salary history or expectations until you are sure of the employer's interest.

- Be prepared to reveal your past salary or history at some point in the interview process. But by postponing the discussion, you have more control. Once you feel there is a sincere interest or an offer is forthcoming, you will be on firmer ground to discuss compensation.

**What does your resume project?**

Your resume can be a powerful tool in conveying your expected salary range—even without explicitly stating how much you make. Make sure your skills, experience, and accomplishments are presented in such a way that a hiring manager could get a fairly reasonable idea of what someone with your background earns per year.

## Describe your ideal work environment?

When hiring managers ask about your ideal work environment, they're trying to figure out if you'll be a good fit for the job and the organization. Here's what they want to hear.

People are happiest and most productive when they work in an environment that suits them. By the same token, companies have different personalities, so it's important for them to hire people who will fit in.

Many job seekers stumble when asked in an interview to describe their ideal work environment. Remember, when you're interviewing, you are being screened for a certain skill set and cultural fit. Here are someq tips on how to formulate your answer to this job interview question.

## Small vs. large companies

A very common question is whether you are most productive and comfortable in a small or large company. Both have benefits, so you need to think about which environment best suits you and your work style. If you like small companies, you might say, "I want to work for a small company because you get exposed to more things faster."

However, if you like the greater resources and more formalized training of a large organization, you should communicate that when interviewing.

Your preference may also depend on where you are in your career. If you're just starting out, a large company may be the place to learn processes. If that's how you feel, say, "I want to own my own company someday and want to learn the best methodologies for running a business."

If you have a number of years under your belt and believe you already know how to manage all or part of a business successfully, then a small company might be the place for you. In your answer, you might say, "I've had great training from large companies and want to import those practices into a small company, so I can have a greater impact."

Typical interview questions like a small company versus a large company are designed to determine where you will be best suited to perform and contribute. Let the interviewer know why you prefer one environment over another.

**Formal vs. informal**

Of the most typical interview questions, this one is designed to illuminate the environment in which you like to work. Everyone has a preferred way of working. Some people like the formality of processes. If that's you, say, "I like when processes are in place, so I know what steps to take."

Others may prefer a more informal work environment in which there is less structure in the way the company operates. If that's your preferred environment, you might say you like extemporaneous meetings in hallways and business decisions made over a casual lunch.

## Work-life balance

How you respond to this question may be a litmus test for how well you'll fit into the organization. For some people, the ideal work environment has set hours, with people arriving at 9 a.m. and leaving at 5 p.m. For those with family responsibilities, this may represent the ideal environment. If this is what you want to convey, you could say, "I think it's important to be productive by 9 a.m., so I can feel good about leaving at 5 p.m."

For others, work is their life, so their ideal environment is one in which most of the other employees feel the same way. If that's you, you might say, "When I'm on a roll, I like to work late, so I like it when there are other peoplearound."

Many people like an environment where they can work remotely, while others prefer the interactions that can happen only at the office. Work-life balance is a typical interview question, so you should give it a great deal of thought because your work environment will have many implications for your long-term happiness.

**Mission statement**

Some companies look for people who share their values and may expect you to address that in your interview. Review the company's mission statement to understand how it addresses its long-term goals and the way it does business. Let the interviewer know how the company's mission reflects your values. You might say, "I want to work for a company that cares about the environment, and that's why I'm so interested in this opportunity."

We all spend the bulk of our day at work, so making sure the work environment is right for you is critical. When interviewing, spend a few minutes describing your ideal environment, so both sides can make an informed decision.

**Know what you want**

The perfect job looks different for every single person, so knowing what you're looking for in an employer will go a long way in helping you find a satisfying job.

**How do you handle working with people who annoy you?**

Get this job interview question right, and maybe you'll find yourself in a new job with less annoying co-workers.

It may sound like a question from an online dating profile, but when job interviewers ask what irritates you about others, they're trying to assess how you will get along with your colleagues and clients, and how your personality will fit in with the company culture.

Think about it. Almost every company has that one worker who types like their fingers are hammers. Or who is a chatterbox? Or who's excruciatingly perky and chipper at all hours. Or who argues with their significant other on the phone loud enough for the entire floor to hear—daily.

Annoying co-workers are a fact of life. They mean no harm, but they can drive you batty, which can make doing your actual job a lot more difficult than it needs to be. Still, you have to push through the annoyance and get your work done. Interviewers want to know you won't let a little thing like a loud chewer sabotages your duties as an employee.

This is not a trick question. Hiring managers are trying to determine first, if you're easily irritated, and second if you're irritated by the habits of their existing staff. They want to know if you're adaptable and a good fit for their organization.

Makes sense, no? But to ensure you don't answer this uestion by unloading every habit you find annoying in others, you need to do some preparation. Use the following tips to focus your answer on something that won't scare off a prospective employer.

### Be upfront about what bothers you

Think of all the different types of personalities that exist in a single workplace. Then consider that everyone is annoyed by something, and when the pressures of work begin to mount, the irritations can start to interfere with teamwork and productivity.

Don't play dumb and tell the interviewer you never get annoyed with anyone. Even the most patient people will find themselves frustrated with co-workers at one point or another, so you need to describe a moment when you've been legitimately annoyed at work. (It likely won't take you too long to come up with something.)

You can cite some things that are genuinely irritating, for example, employee's taking credit for your work.

You say: "It doesn't happen often, but I really get irritated when one person hogs all the glory on something that was a group effort.

I believe in giving credit where it is due and fairness within a team dynamic."

## Show you aren't bothered by the little stuff

Legitimate grievances are different from personal peeves; in the grand scheme of things, someone who bites their nails is less of an issue than someone who misses every single deadline given to them. Employers don't want to hire people who are going to be irritated by every little thing, so you need to give an answer that shows the little stuff won't get to you.

Working with others is challenging. People who are easily irritated are difficult to work with, and people who deal with their concerns with others don't create more issues down the road.

Also, you want to avoid sounding like you aren't able to work with people who operate differently than you do.qIt's way too easy to fall into the trap of answering this uestion by showing a lack of patience or understanding toward others.

Maybe you're most productive in the mornings, but your co- worker really picks up in the afternoon. This shouldn't derail the team. You need to adapt to different working styles, otherwise, you're the annoying one.

You say: "I'm bothered by big mistakes or problems that have team impact. For example, it would bother me greatly if a co- worker were to miss an important deadline for a team project. It's unfair to the people in the group who made their deadlines."

## Demonstrate your patience when handling annoyance

Lastly, you must demonstrate that you handle your annoyances in a calm and productive manner. Nobody likes a complainer who doesn't take any action to fix the situation.

Most interviewers are seeking to understand if the person being interviewed is positive and solutions-based, as well as a strong communicator. It is important not to be too harsh or too much of a people pleaser.

Meaning, shouting or putting down someone is both rude and unhelpful, no matter how annoying they are. Instead, it's best to explain how you listen to others when there's a misunderstanding. Give an answer that shows you prefer to discuss your irritations and find a point of agreement with others, rather than simply remaining annoyed or running to the boss to whine without first attempting to solve the issue yourself.

Describe a healthy way to handle that situation, such as, confronting the employee and only alerting your supervisor if needed.

You say: "Because I know I get irritated when co-workers miss deadlines, I try to always make sure goals are clearly communicated to everyone on the team. I also like to implement regular check-ins to make sure we're all on the same page, rather than waiting until the end to see if there's a problem. If the deadline is missed anyway,

I try to find out what I can do differently next time so the problem doesn't repeat itself."

## Smile—you're not done yet

It's not easy to get along with difficult people, but in the workplace, you have no choice if you want to keep—in this case get—a job. Showing hiring managers that you're good- natured are a step in the right direction, and you want your other answers to back up that claim. From "Why should we hire you?" to "What's your biggest weakness?" Hiring managers are looking for you to demonstrate congeniality as well as compelling answers.

## Answering Scenario Questions

You may also be given scenario questions such as "If a client asks you to deliver the product and it will not be ready in time, how would you respond?"

These questions are not usually asked in the hope of getting an exact response, but more aimed at seeing how you think.

They may also be trying to assess your behavioral patterns. You may even be asked how you have handled these situations in the past.

There are no perfect answers, so the best way to respond is, to be honest, and present your answers in a positive light. Be clear and concise and avoid being vague at all costs.

**Things recruiters say should be in a thank-you note**

This is your last chance to make a good impression. Use it wisely.

If you've reached the stage of your job search where you're sending thank-you notes, you're almost at the finish line— but don't get complacent. A thank-you note is a critical opportunity to seal the deal, so you need to get it right.

## 1. The words "thank you"

"Thank-you notes should be sincere and should tell the interview team why their time invested was well worth it. It is not a time to name drop or schmooze with insincere general comments. These thank-you notes get thrown away."

Heather Kinzie, owner of A Leading Solution in Anchorage, Alaska.

## 2. Sincerity

"Genuine notes are the best notes, and I save them for my smile file, to look back at on days that aren't so great to remind myself why I do what I do," says Kristina Minyard, a corporate recruiter in Huntsville, Alabama.

## 3. A bit about what you learned

"I like it when a candidate specifically mentions something they learned about our company while interviewing and how excited they are about that new piece of information."

— Kristina Minyard

## 4. Enthusiasm for the job

"This is a very important step, and yet many candidates overlook it. Tell your interviewer, again, that you are interested in working there, and why: 'I'd be delighted to join XYZ Company.' Be specific." —Tammy Colson, owner of TalentCrib in Cleveland.

## 5. Reasons why you'll be a great fit

"I like to see that a person has thought about the job as described in the interview and reiterate bothq their interest in the position and an ability to tie their ualifications to the role." —Mary Faulkner, head of talent for Denver Water in Colorado

## 6. Something new about you

"I like to see something not revealed qin the interview. The thank-you note should include a new uestion or point you missed mentioning when we spoke. This shows you put some thought into your responses even after you left. If it's missing, that's a red flag." —Mike Smith, founder of Salescoaching1 in Windermere, Florida

## 7. Proof the conversation stayed with you

"It's great to see specific references to the discussion that took place in the interview. This demonstrates an attention to detail and a recollection of the specific conversation." —

Frank Zupan, director of talent management for Associated Materials in Cleveland

## 8. Why you think we're great

"Tell me that you like or are impressed with the people you talked with. Tell me something that shows you understand why we think we're special. If you can demonstrate positivity and an appreciation of our culture, that goes a long way." — Lisa Kaminski, talent engagement director for Engage Partners in Cincinnati

## 9. Correct spelling

"I like seeing my name spelled correctly. It's Erin, not Eric. And Stevens, not Stephens. Details matter." —Erin Stevens, corporate recruiter with MasterBrand Cabinets in Louisville, Kentucky

**Job search etiquette**

A thank-you note is just one of the pieces that make up the job search puzzle. You must get a hiring manager's attention, display your skills and experience, and demonstrate the value you'd bring to a company. Yeah—all of that.

# CHAPTER 6

# BEST QUESTIONS TO ASK AT THE END OF A JOB INTERVIEW

An interview is a two-way street. Your potential employer is asking you questions to learn about you and your skills. In return, you need to prepare questions to ask your potential employer about the position, your boss, and the company in order to be sure that this is the right job for you.

In addition, if you don't prepare smart questions, you run the risk of the interviewer assuming you aren't interestedor haven't prepared.

Your opportunity to ask questions usually comes at the end of the interview. You must prepare at least two questions that demonstrate your interest in the position, your drive to excel in the role, and the fact that you've done some homework (researched company, industry, department).

So how do you come up with these smart questions that show you're the perfect hire? As you conduct your pre-interview research, make note of topics that you'd like to ask about.

Keep in mind that the best questions to ask are focused, open- ended question.

Avoid yes or no questions and avoid questions that are so broad that they are difficult to answer. You don't want to stump the interviewer when you're trying to make a good impression and develop rapport.

**Still not sure what to ask? Here are proven examples of good questions to ask during a job interview:**

**Can you tell me more about the day-to-day responsibilities of this job?**

This is your chance to learn as much as possible about the role so you can decide whether this is a job you really want. By learning more about the day-to-day tasks, you will also gain more insight into what specific skills and strengths are needed and you can address any topics that haven't already been covered.

## What do you think are the most important qualities for someone to excel in this role?

This question can often lead to valuable information that's not in the job description. It can help you learn about the company culture and expectations so you can show that you are a good fit.

## What are your expectations for this role during the first 30 days, 60 days, year?

Find out what your employer's expectations are for the person in this position.

## Describe the culture of the company.

Are you a good fit for this particular organization? Make sure you are comfortable with the culture and the dynamic of the company.

## Where do you think the company is headed in the next 5 years?

If you plan to be in this role for several years, make sure the company is growing so you can grow with the company.

**Who do you consider your top competitor, and why?**

You should already have an idea of the company's major competitors, but it can be useful to ask your interviewer for their thoughts. Naturally, they will be able to give you the insight you can't find anywhere else.

**What are the biggest opportunities facing the company/ department right now?**

This question shows your drive to seize the opportunity and may help you learn more about where the company will be focusing over the next several months.

**What are the biggest challenges facing the company/ department right now?**

On the flip side, you may want to ask about challenges. This question can help you uncover trends and issues in the industry and perhaps identify areas where your skills could save the day.

**What do you like best about working for this company?**

Ask about your interviewer's personal experience for additional insight into the company's culture.

**What is the typical career path for someone in this role?**

This question can help you learn whether the company promotes from within, and how career advancementq works within the organization. By asking the uestion, you show your interest in growing with the organization — just be careful not to phrase it in a way that sounds too self-serving (i.e. When can I expect a raise and a promotion?).

**How do I compare with the other candidates you've interviewed for this role?**

This is a slightly risky choice. You don't want to put the interviewer in an awkward position. However, if things are going well and you've built a strong rapport, this question can help you see if there are any concerns or issues that you could address to show why you're the best person for the job.

# What Are The Next Steps In The Interview Process?

This question shows that you are eager to move forward in the process. It will also help you gain important information about the timeline for hiring so that you can follow up appropriately.

Remember: Don't ask about salary or benefits just yet. Wait until you are in the final steps of the interview process to negotiate with the hiring manager or an HR representative.

**Your Questions – Their Answers**

Asking questions of the person interviewing you serves two purposes. Firstly it will tell you what you need to know about the company and the job. Secondly, it will show your enthusiasm and interest in the job. Many of your questions should be in response to what they are saying as it will show you are listening. Having no questions or response would suggest that you either do not understand or are not paying attention. For example, a response to "you will be dealing directly with clients" maybe "will that be over the phone or in person?

In general, other typical questions may include:

- Can you tell me more about the day-to-day duties?
- How has this position become vacant?
- Can you give me more detail on the company?
- What would be my main responsibilities?
- What are the prospects for promotion?
- What training will I be given?
- What are the future plans for the company?
- Who will I report to?
- Would it be possible to see more of the Company?

## Things To Avoid

- Do not be over chatty. If you talk too much in an interview they will be concerned about you being over chatty in the workplace.
- Do not heavily criticise previous employers. No matter how justified, you will just come over as a malcontent.
- Do not make your first question about the holiday or sick pay.
- Never show aggression or frustration and never argue with the person interviewing you.

- Do not argue with or criticize the way the company works.
- Don't show lack of interest through your body language. Look at the person speaking to you, react to what they say and don't fidget.

# How To Finish The Interview

When the interview is coming to a close, it is a good psychology to finish on a positive note. If you feel an interview has gone well, there is nothing to be lost by asking "do you feel I could be of interest to your company?" If the answer is "No" it would probably always have been a "No" regardless. If they feel you could be suited, they will likely answer "Yes" and if this is the last thing they say to you it will be the last thing they remember. You can also ask the question "when could you expect to hear from them?" as this may avoid a more delayed response. Statistically, the more someone delays making a decision the more likely it will be a "No".

## The Follow Up

Another way of showing your enthusiasm is with a follow-up call to the interview. The interviewer will usually give an indication of when you should hear feedback, if not... it is acceptable to call a few days later (although not less than four days). The sensible approach would be one of a proactive candidate, keen on the job rather than an impatient candidate demanding to know what is happening. Under no circumstances sound pushy or aggressive as this may induce a negative response.

# FINALLY...

When all is said and done, your overall personality will play a large part in the selection process. In most cases, the person interviewing you will be your future boss. If they like you as a person they are more likely to want to work with you.

Prior to leaving make sure that you have noted the name of the person or persons who interviewed you. This will come in handy later for a number of purposes. Also, do make sure that you shake hands once again with your interviewer and thank them for taking the time to meet with you. Also, it's not out of line to ask when they expect to be making a decision. This gives you a timeline to go by.

Always be sure to send a thank-you letter. This practice not only demonstrates good social eti uette but it also helps to keep you and your skills fresh in the mind of the interviewer. On some occasions an interviewer already has an idea by the time the interviews are completed who they will be calling to offer the job; however, on many more occasions, they still remain unsure who will be awarded that coveted slot. Sometimes they want a little time to 'sleep' on the decision or they may need to consult supervisors or others within their organization regarding the hiring decision. If a decision has not already been reached in the mind of the employer when all of the interviews have been completed, taking the time to send a thank-you letter can go a long way toward making sure you don't get lost in the shuffle.

While it's a good idea to send a polite thank you note to the person who interviewed you it is not a good idea to pester that person to no end. The only result you are likely to achieve through this strategy is alienating yourself from them and assuring that you won't get the job. Although 'don't take no for an answer' is a strategy that many aggressive job coaches recommend; it is still always best to observe polite social standards.

That is not to say that you should sit by the phone and allow several weeks to elapse, waiting, while you hear nothing and do nothing. Ideally, your thank you letter should have gone out the same day as the interview, no later than the following day. This means that the interviewer should receive it within one to two days following the initial interview.

Keep track of when the employer indicated a decision would be made and if that time has come and gone, it is perfectly permissible to go ahead and phone them. However; when you do make the call, be polite. State your name, the date you interviewed and the position for which you interviewed. You may say that you are following up to in uire as to whether a decision has been made.

At this point, the conversation can go a number of ways. The employer may indicate that a decision has been made and all candidates who were not selected will be receiving a letter in the mail. If this is the response you receive, it is your cue that you were not hired. Had you been, you would have received a phone call from the employer by now.

Thank them for their times, ask them to keep you in mind for any future vacancies and get off the line. Don't burn any bridges. It could be that there was simply a better- qualified candidate for that particular position, but they might consider you for a different, future position.

On the other hand, the employer may state that they are still reviewing the resumes, conducting interviews, etc, etc. This type of response could mean a couple of different things. It could mean that they really have made a decision and the person just doesn't feel comfortable telling you on the phone that you weren't selected or it could simply be taken at face value.

Perhaps something came up and their initial timeline has been forced to be extended somewhat. In either case, always remain polite and thank them for their time. After you end the call, make a note of the date on your planner and set a tickler to remind yourself to call back in a week if you still haven't heard anything. Call back once a week, every week until a decision is made. Once a week is persistent; a trait which is to be admired. Once a day is pesky; a trait that should be avoided at all costs.

While it can be difficult to wait around after the interview, the most important two things that you should do is not blow the opportunity by annoying the employer with numerous pesky phone calls and by all means do not show up announced at their office door asking if they have arrived at a decision. Finally, make sure that you don't pin all your hopes on one job. Yes, it may have been your first choice and your ideal dream job; however; this is probably also true for someone else as well. Use the time while you are waiting to hear back from the employer to line up your

'B' plan. Continue job searching, scheduling interviews and most importantly , reminding yourself that you can do this.

The job market is extremely tough but not impossible. Companies are all looking for the right candidate and you need to make sure you have the edge to show you are that person. With a great resume and effective interview, you will be able to sell yourself. You will be able to stand out without looking overconfident.

I hope that this eBook has given you some clear instructions on how to face all types of interviews with ease and professionalism. Once you master the interview, you can achieve confidence and success in the job field.

Good luck, now it's up to you.

# ABOUT THE AUTHOR PAGE

Ernest is a director, interview coach and CV Makeover consultant of CV Interview Services with over 7 years of experience in interview coaching, CV makeover and writing supporting statement for job candidates and university applicants. Ernest first priority is customer satisfaction and the success rate is very high based on a referral. Thus, he delivers high- quality services to all range of clients, and the type of service required is tailored to individual needs or requirements. Go to his website: www.cvinterviewservices.com For a range of services tailored to individual needs.

His book is available on the following Amazon page: —

**HOW TO BE SUCCESSFUL AT INTERVIEWS:**

https://www.amazon.co.uk/dp/B07F6LC3Y6

Made in the USA
Coppell, TX
28 March 2021

52565134R00059